The
Farm
Colouring
Book

Buster Books

ILLUSTRATED BY CHRIS DICKASON

EDITED BY EMMA TAYLOR
DESIGNED BY DERRIAN BRADDER
COVER DESIGN BY ANGIE ALLISON

First published in Great Britain in 2021 by Buster Books,
an imprint of Michael O'Mara Books Limited, 9 Lion Yard,
Tremadoc Road, London SW4 7NQ

W www.mombooks.com/buster   F Buster Books   🐦 @BusterBooks   📷 @buster_books

A CIP catalogue record for this book is available from the British Library.

ISBN: 978-1-78055-760-1

1 3 5 7 9 10 8 6 4 2

This book was printed in July 2021 by Leo Paper Products Ltd,
Heshan Astros Printing Limited, Xuantan Temple Industrial Zone,
Gulao Town, Heshan City, Guangdong Province, China.

FSC
www.fsc.org

MIX
Paper from
responsible sources
FSC® C020056